RUBANK EDUCATIONAL LIBRARY No. 46

RUBANK

Elementary METHOD

BASSOON

J. E. SKORNICKA

A FUNDAMENTAL COURSE FOR INDIVIDUAL
OR LIKE-INSTRUMENT CLASS INSTRUCTION

HAL•LEONARD®
CORPORATION
7777 W. BLUEMOUND RD. P.O. BOX 13819 MILWAUKEE, WI 53213

LESSON 1

Introduction

The basic theory underlying the organization plan of this course is, that good instrumental performance depends on the pupil being able to hear the desired pitch before attempting to produce it. Practically all passages in this course should, therefore, be sung properly as to pitch and intonation before being played on the instrument.

Correlating the voice training which the child recieves in the daily singing classes with the playing of an instrument, particularly in the manner of pitch conception, should be emphasized. Pupils should be made to realize that the two processes of training are alike with the exception that the instrument is substituted for the vocal organs in the production of a tone.

To produce as beautiful a tone as possible is quite important, but to be able to play in pitch and with good intonation, should be a major objective.

Developing the ear beyond the technical performance of the pupil generally insures faster musical growth, whereas the development of tone and technic is a matter of time, during which the embouchure will develop and the ear will become more discriminating as to the quality of tone being produced.

J. E. SKORNICKA

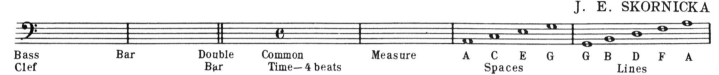

| Bass Clef | Bar | Double Bar | Common Time—4 beats | Measure | A C E G Spaces | G B D F A Lines |

Whole Note and Whole Rest Study

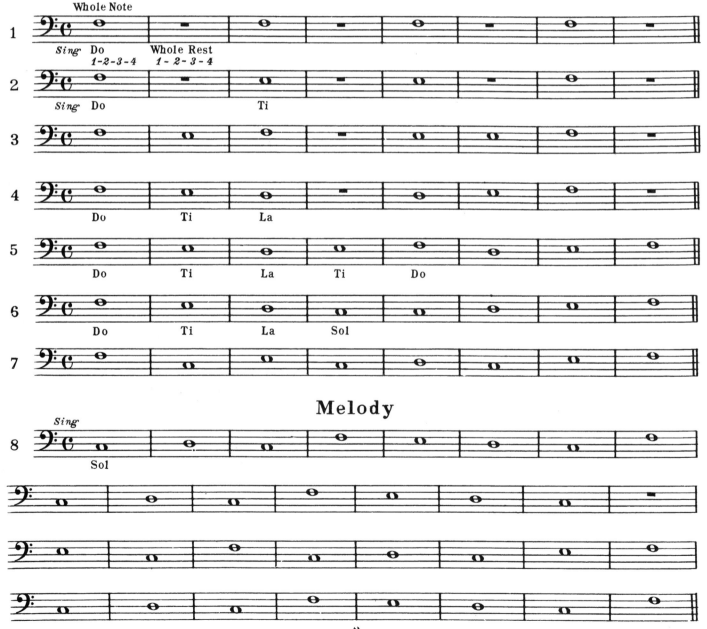

Melody

Elem. Meth. for Bassoon

1 - 2 - 3 - 4   1 - 2   3 - 4   1 - 2   B   A   G

Half Notes and Half Rests

Sing

1   Do

2   1 - 2 3 - 4

Counting Study

3

4

Melody

5

New Notes

Sing

6   Do Ti Do

7   Do

8

9

Chord Study

10

★ Note   Explanation of First Line of Each Lesson

The first line of each lesson is a review of old problems and the introduction of new ones. Each one of these lines should be thoroughly gone through before proceeding with the lesson proper. The new problems should be clearly explained by the teacher, and review problems clearly explained by the pupil. The pupil should be able to distinguish the review from the new.

Quarter Notes   Quarter Rest   Repeat

Quarter Note Study

1

1- 2 -3 - 4

Melody

2
1 - 2 - 3 - 4

Technical Study

3

Rhythmic Study

4

Scale Study

5

Practice daily

Difficult Intervals

Octave Study

C Major Chord

C Major Scale

Melody

Come All Ye Faithful

WILLIS

Petite Duet

3/4 Studies

First Waltz

German

Low Tone Study

F Major Chord

F Major Scale

Melody

Rhythmic Study

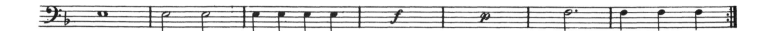

Rhythmic Studies

Duet in F Major

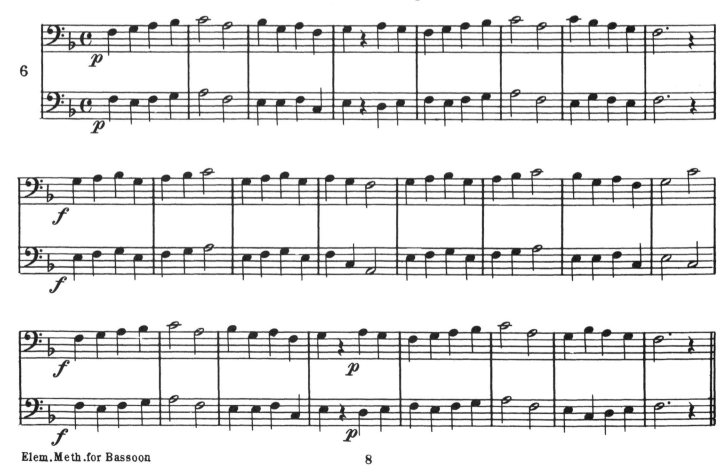

Bb Major Chord Study

Bb Major Scale

Bb Scale Study

High-Note Study

Progress Duet

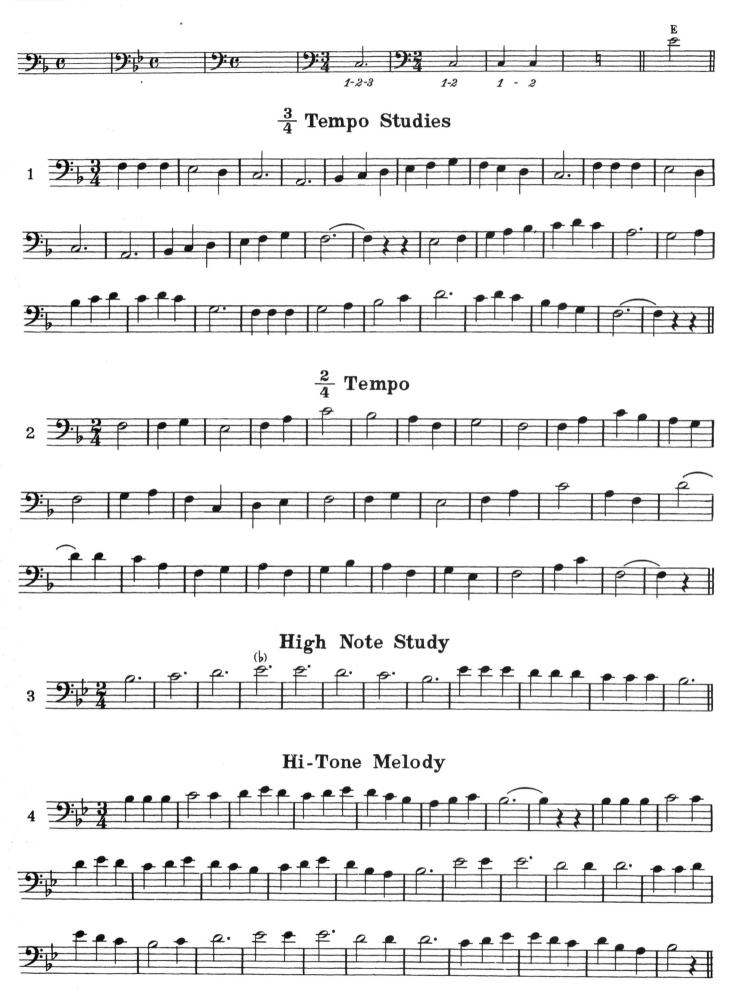

$\frac{3}{4}$ Tempo Studies

$\frac{2}{4}$ Tempo

High Note Study

Hi-Tone Melody

Tie   Slur

Slur Studies

Petite Waltz

Eighth - Note Studies

Long Long Ago

Folk-Song

German

F Major Chord (2 octaves)

F Major Scale (2 octaves)

Rhythmic Study
From Surprise Symphony

HAYDN

F Major Scale Study

Petite Gavotte

Dotted Quarter Notes

America

Rhythmic Patterns

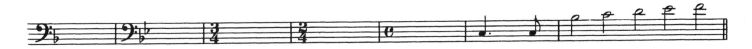

Dotted Quarter Notes
AULD LANG SYNE

Onward Christian Soldiers

Classic Duet

G Major Chord

G Major Scale

Melody in G Major

Slur Study

Rhythmic Duet

Technical Etudes

Chords—Analysed

Difficult Interval Studies

Alla Breve Study

Melody

Theme Symphony No. 1

BRAHMS

Sixteenth Notes

Sixteenth Rest

Sixteenth Note Studies

Melody

Scale Articulations

C Major

F Major

B♭ Major

Chord Articulation

$\frac{2}{4}$ Rhythms

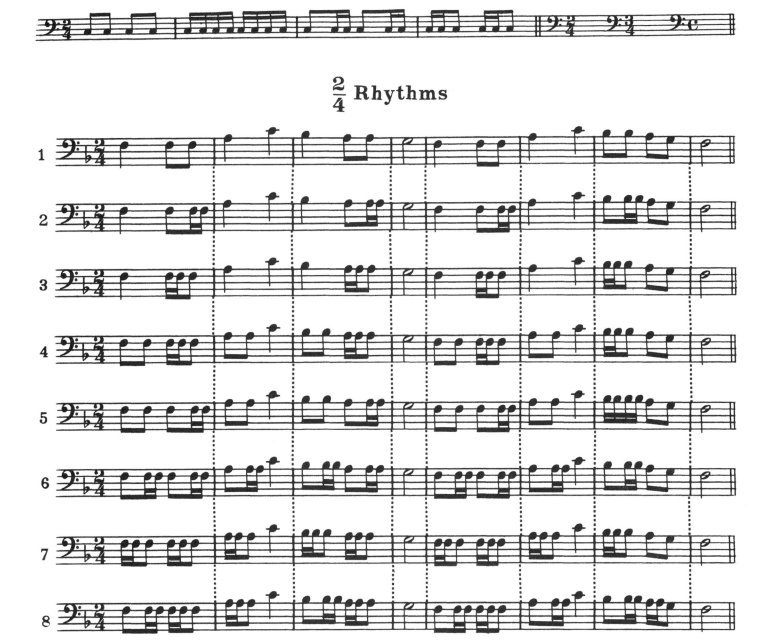

Folk Song

Dotted Eighth Note Studies

Melody

Maryland My Maryland

Love's Old Sweet Song

Name the Keys.

Duet

1

Low Tone Study

2

Octave Study

3

$\frac{6}{8}$ Tempo

$\frac{6}{8}$ Tempo Variations

Eb Major Chord

Eb Major Scale

Technical Study in Eb

Blue Bells of Scotland

E♭ Major Studies

De Capua

D.C. — To the Beginning   f — Fortissimo   ff — Mezzo forte   mf — Mezzo piano   mp

D Major Chord

1

D Major Scale

2

(♯)

Melody in D Major

3

Petite Duet

Moderato

4

mf

mf

Fine

Fine

f

f

p

p

D.C.

D.C.

Technical Etudes

Melody in Two Tempos

New $\frac{6}{8}$ Rhythms

Technical Study

G Major Scale

Chord Study

Syncopation

Melody

Syncopated Melody

Triplet Study

Triplet Study

From Tannhauser

Andante

WAGNER

Technical Etudes

Difficult Interval Studies

Tenor Clef

Tenor Clef may be placed on any portion of staf, indicating Middle C.

Most commonly used   Treble Clef

Study in Change of Clef

Enharmonic Chart. Line (a) Familiar Tones. Line (b) same pitch and same fingering as Line (a).

Composite Enharmonic Chart

Chromatic Scales

Chromatic Etude

Minor Scales and Studies

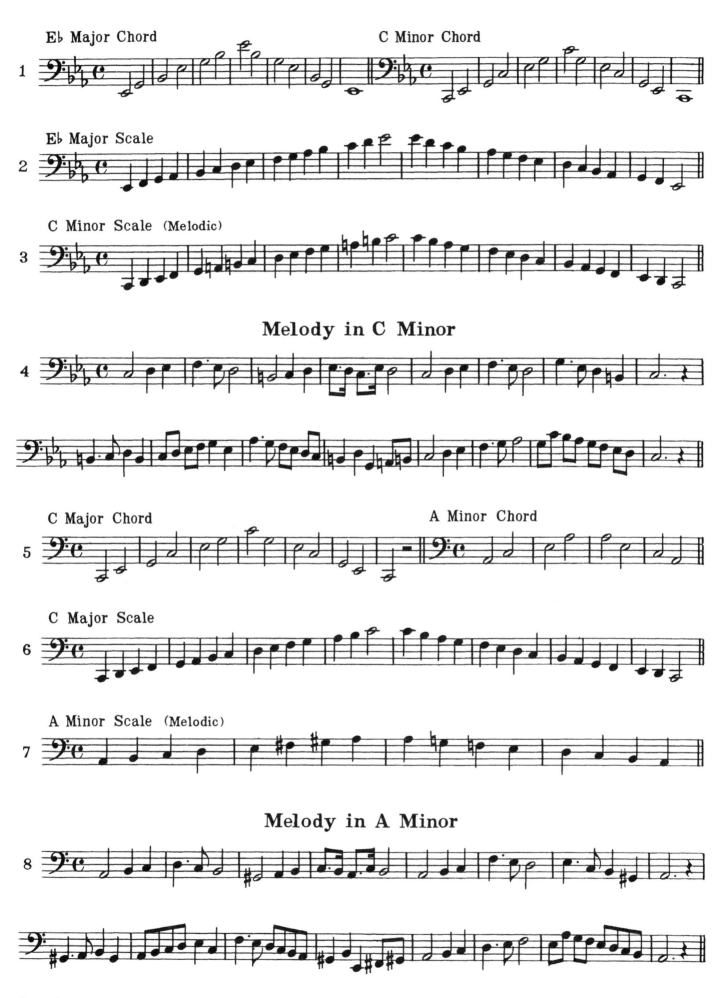

Eb Major Chord

C Minor Chord

Eb Major Scale

C Minor Scale (Melodic)

Melody in C Minor

C Major Chord

A Minor Chord

C Major Scale

A Minor Scale (Melodic)

Melody in A Minor

Chromatic Studies

Where only a half step separates two successive natural tones, the lower one sharped will sound the upper tone and the upper one flated will sound the lower tone.

Two tones which only a half step separates in the natural scale, will be marked with brackets thus ⌐¬ ∟⌐ in the following ascending natural range of the instrument.

(♯) Sharp raises the pitch of a tone ½ step.　(x) Double sharp raises the pitch of a tone 2 half steps.
(♭) Flat lowers the pitch of a tone ½ step.　(♭♭) Double flat lowers the pitch of a tone 2 half steps.

Same Chromatic Scale in Different Keys

Additional Scales

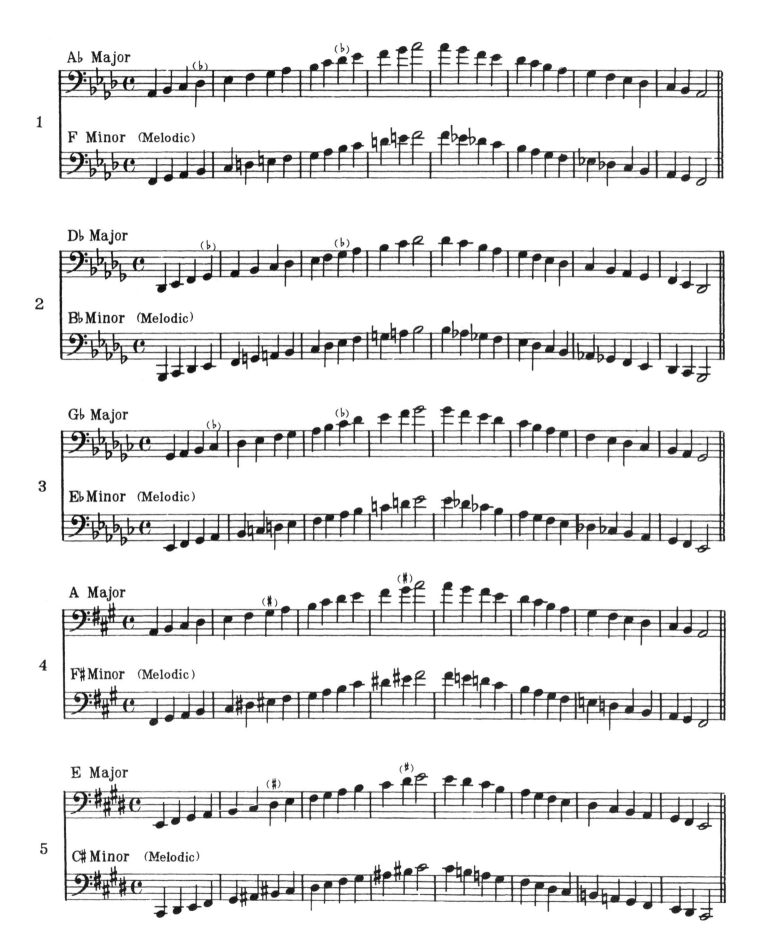

Examination Study
First Half Year

Examination Study
Second Half Year

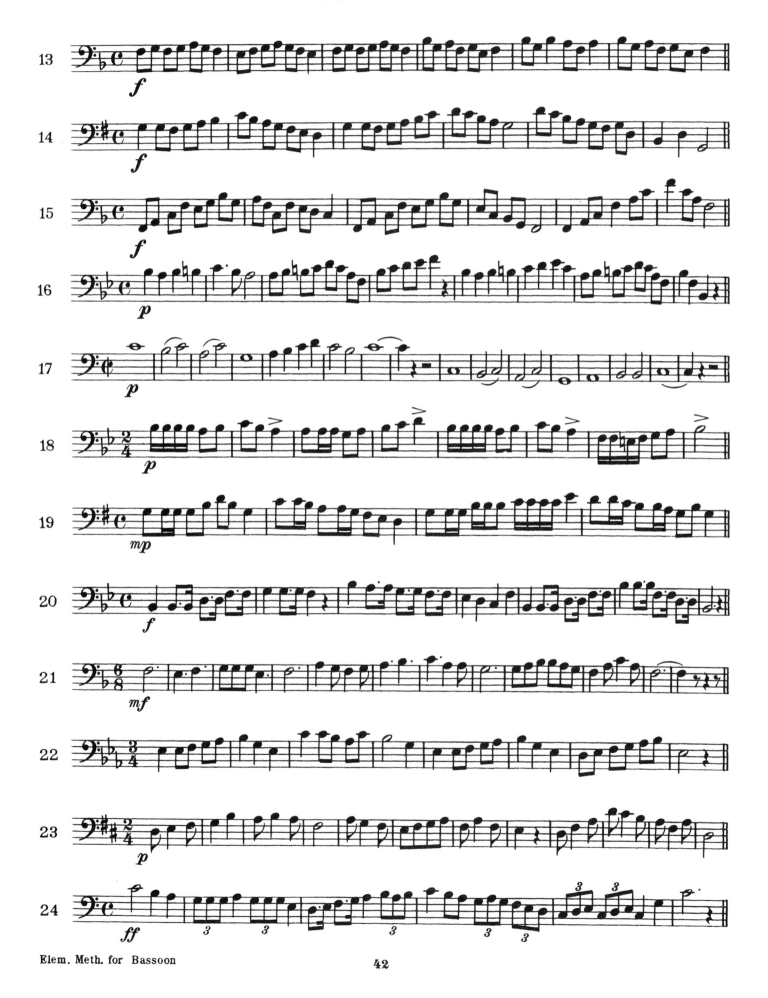

Building Major Scales

The pattern for all major scales is the same. In scales, there are intervals or spaces between tones which are either whole steps or half steps. A whole step will be known as 1 an a half step will be known as ½ .

In major scales the ½ steps always occur between the 3rd and 4th steps (mi-fa) and between the 7th and 8th steps (ti-do)

The first 4 tones of a scale are known as the lower tetrachord and the upper 4 tones as the upper tetrachord.

A whole step must separate the two tetrachords.

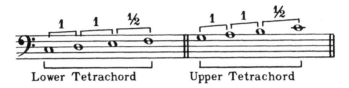

Lower Tetrachord   Upper Tetrachord

Pattern for major scales 1 - 1 - ½ ‖ 1 - 1 - ½ .

In building scales start on any tone and write out 8 successive tones, and then adjust, by means of sharps and flats, the tones of each tetrachord according to the major scale pattern 1 - 1 - ½ ‖ 1 - 1 - ½ .

Example: add sharps or flats necessary to fit pattern.

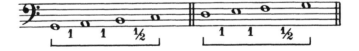

Add sharps or flats necessary to fit pattern.

BUILDING MELODIC MINOR SCALES

Melodic minor scales must be built to fit pattern as shown above. Pattern 1 - ½ - 1‖ 1 - 1 - ½ .

German Folk Song

Polish Folk Song

Carry Me Back To Old Virginny

BLAND

Alma Mater

Old American

Lullaby

BRAHMS

Gavotte

Bassoon Theme from Jupiter Symphony

MOZART

Theme from Symphony No. 8

BEETHOVEN

Theme from Symphony No. 8